an evening absence
still waiting for moon

an evening absence
still waiting for moon

Bruce Kauffman

First Edition

Hidden Brook Press
www.HiddenBrookPress.com
writers@HiddenBrookPress.com

Copyright © 2019 Hidden Brook Press
Copyright © 2019 Bruce Kauffman

All rights for poems revert to the author. All rights for book, layout and design remain with Hidden Brook Press. No part of this book may be reproduced except by a reviewer who may quote brief passages in a review. The use of any part of this publication reproduced, transmitted in any form or by any means, electronic, mechanical, photocopied, recorded or otherwise stored in a retrieval system without prior written consent of the publisher is an infringement of the copyright law.

an evening absence still waiting for moon
by Bruce Kauffman

Editor – John B. Lee
Cover Photo – Ali Dixon
Cover Design – Richard M. Grove
Layout and Design – Richard M. Grove

Typeset in Garamond
Printed and bound in Canada
Distributed in USA by Ingram
       in Canada by Hidden Brook Distribution

Library and Archives Canada Cataloguing in Publication

Title: An evening absence still waiting for moon / Bruce Kauffman.

Names: Kauffman, Bruce, 1950- author.

Description: Poems.

Identifiers: Canadiana 20190076577 | ISBN 9781927725689 (softcover)

Classification: LCC PS8621.A685 E93 2019 | DDC C811/.6—dc23

Ancient World

Orange sunset
In the deep shell of summer
A long silence reaching
Across the dry pastures
In the distance a dog barks
At the sound of a door closing
And at once I am older

W.S. Merwin from
(The Moon before Morning,
Copper Canyon Press, 2015)

Contents:

– early morning – *p. 1*
– a calling – *p. 2*
– a life reminder – *p. 3*
– last poem – *p. 4*
– morning lake – *p. 5*
– insulation – *p. 6*
– hollow tree – *p. 8*
– universes – *p. 10*
– to fully be – *p. 11*
– lost again – *p. 12*
– the end of day – *p. 14*
– canada – *p. 15*
– divided time – *p. 16*
– poem – *p. 17*
– the living and the dead – *p. 18*
– near the end – *p. 22*
– voice – *p. 23*
– origin – *p. 24*
– a long-ago memory revisited – *p. 26*
– veil of day – *p. 29*
– the full of you – *p. 30*
– waterways – *p. 31*
– downtown – may 9th – *p. 32*
– sliver – *p. 34*
– a winter landscape – *p. 35*
– when asked on your road to silence – *p. 38*
– on learning – *p. 40*
– pulse – *p. 41*
– light snow – *p. 42*
– invisible – *p. 43*
– needs no definition – *p. 44*

– fear – *p. 45*
– a café in time – *p. 46*
– this late in autumn   an elegy – *p. 48*
– passing – *p. 51*
– a murder of crows – *p. 52*
– within a day – *p. 54*
– in whispered language of ash and bone – *p. 56*
– rising tides – *p. 57*
– poets – *p. 58*
– moving through light and darkness – *p. 59*
– this evening – *p.60*
– almost winter – *p. 62*
– stream – *p. 63*
– midwinter – *p. 64*
– languages – *p. 65*
– again on aging – *p. 66*
– what i mostly am – *p. 67*
– from last night – *p. 68*
– gardens – *p. 69*
– how – *p. 70*
– here – p. 71
– the languages of history – *p. 72*
– in that hidden garden behind – *p. 73*
– in the end – *p. 74*
– on this shore – *p. 76*

About the Author – *p. 79*
About the Front Cover Photographer – *p. 81*

early morning

early morning

the day already
growing
        into itself

each second now
rolling into and
then slipping away

we are already
history becoming

in this endless
        cosmic breath

a calling

the walk not taken

a choice
        instead
to stand beside
my outside door

a slow crescent moon
        directly above
points its lower tip
toward a single star
in an almost dark
and empty sky

tonight
in this slow
season ending

the next even
slower to begin

i, along with
        the season
        the star
        the moon
        the empty black sky
attempting each
        all
to find our own way
back home

a life reminder
haiku to self on rising

before there can be
shadow there must be always
first a present light

last poem

when will i know
in the writing
that my last poem
      is written

will it simply be
when the pen
runs out of ink

or will it be when
the last tree
      is felled

and in the tears
of that time

nothing to write

no one to tell

A slightly modified version of this poem was originally created in response to a piece of fibre artwork by Janet Elliot and hung beside it in the 2014 Kingston WritersFest 'Stitch and Stanza' collaborative display featuring a group of poets and fibre artists.

morning lake

the still lake
        this morning
as liquid and
as fluid as mirror

becomes it

insulation

how to insulate myself
      from the noise
      of the day

      from the echoing shouts
      of history

how to distance myself
from the pompousness of logic
      the world never becoming
      deaf to that noise

two men sit beside me
in their too loud
too long too proud
conversations
between the pages
of their newspapers

newspapers

only telling them
what happened
      yesterday

while a new morning
      away from this
is spinning outside

already weaving itself
in the still colour and fullness
of what it is
      becoming

it has lost them
they are lost to it

tomorrow morning
with their papers in hand
they will read about
        a short remnant of a single
        small thread of the full
        blanket of this day

and they will look up
from their papers

they will talk about it
loudly and long

and tell themselves
that they know
while

a new day outside
is weaving its new threads
        into a curtain

to protect itself
        from them

hollow tree
      after W. S. Merwin's 'Touching the Tree'

there is but one tree in the park
with a semi-hollowed out bottom
at the base of its trunk

will this tree fall
not to the weight
        of seasons and wind
but instead behind
the fear-driven
        henchman
with his snarling
        saw

in the end
its fate
its destiny
i do not know
do not want to consider

but today only in this misty rain
of a cold winter late afternoon

that hole
        in the trunk
                a funnel in time

echoing
W. S. Merwin's 'Touching the Tree'

and in it becoming
for me or
        any other small child
a cave

a cave
        before the lion comes

Posted originally on Kingston Frontenac Public Library's
'virtual blackboard', circa 2015.

'Touching the Tree' appeared in Merwin's
'The Rain in the Trees' (Alfred A. Knopf, 1987).

universes

to a single almost invisible
wisp of dew caressing yet
          a high hanging leaf
a full single raindrop just below
still nestled in the hollow
          of a low branch
is an ocean

to fully be

to be at the same time
so completely unfocused
and intuitively aware
that you catch the
most minute shift of light
against any single leaf
        before even
                its shadow does

lost again

there is a forgotten
sky above us

we seldom notice

we forget

we forget
much

        the air brushing over
            around
        the water running
            in rivers beneath
            the crust
                of the earth
            and rolling silently
            just beneath
                our feet

the sky
the water
both going somewhere

    nowhere

they always leading us

but we fail to notice

we always lost
    in ourselves

we always looking

    away

the end of day

with this heavy coat
of routine and obligation
        discarded
and the day at my back

i sit and allow this flush of air
this gentle cool breeze
of all possibility to brush through

any breeze welcome
but this breeze
        this evening
ever more so as it arrives

rides through
my open windows
as i soften to absorb

and here this evening
i realize there is something
beyond happiness
        even joy
higher than
        ecstasy even

and for it there is
no word

but this tonight
        its definition

canada

i've sat on both sides
of the river under two flags
      each accepting
but claiming not the other
the earth claiming
      neither
      both

i once the foreigner here
i the expatriate
the resident now
but claiming allegiance only
      to world and self
with no sense of estrangement

yet here there is a difference

a softer texture
a quieter voice
      a more gentle heart

i am certain that ten thousand
years from today
as they dig up the fossils
of our lives on each side
they will notice the softness
of those here

      and will wonder why

divided time

it is evening here
and in a few slow seconds
the dusk begins to erase itself
off horizon's edge to leave
only the black chalkboard
      of sky

in that exact instant
      on the other side
the world watches
the sun slowly rising
painting the horizon in
its breathtaking colours
      of amber
          burgundy
      and golden red

as if blackness had stolen
all the colours
from our evening sky

caressed them for an instant
between its palms
and then
in a gentle sweep
spread them with its fingers upon
that chalkboard's other side

just above
      below
that ever-edge
of horizon shared

poem

the pen hesitates
in the extraneous noise
of these mundane conversations
in this room
and of those before
past echoes still

this pen yearning again
for a distant music's whisper

the ink within waits
waits   waits
for that right ambient sound
this full breath of day
the right slant of sun
the quiet rebound
of shadow's echo

and then
in an instant's surprise
on that perfect edge
of light touching shadow
of shadow discovering sound
the ink then spills
its long-held breath
across an empty
        waiting page

the living and the dead

for the 'Dia de los Muertos' celebration event
– Kingston, ON - Nov 6, 2016

i.

we come into this world
with nothing

we ride and roll
run and crawl through this life

death
the crossing over
that ever-fine line between
      life and other

a fine line
invisible
      or at least so it seems

perhaps invisible on this side only

we journey through our lives
we memorize we eulogize
we commemorate we celebrate

we laugh we mourn
we fear we rejoice
we sustain ourselves
      and other

in this time between
birth and death
we will leave pieces of
        ourselves

pieces of those pieces
will linger after

each day here
        is a gift
each second in
each day
        a gift more

ii.

allow as each second arrives
the absolute newness in it
lose yourself to its bountiful surprise

carry with you the souls
       of the past
the souls of those
not with us here

with your own eyes let them see again
       vicariously
the full of this day
in its all-encompassing
       wonder

each day is a piece
of the story of your life

each day a page

staple those pages
of your days together

you are a new book
still writing itself

even not yet finished
    complete

and with the last page written
that full book of your life
will be picked up and carried
will be read with the eyes
of both strangers and friends and

then gently placed
on the nightstands
of all those you've touched

near the end

near the end
i will remember
        none of this

and in that time
will ask forgiveness
        for the forgetting

even then not knowing
what was lost

but in the enveloping
        darkness and its wave
        of infinite silence
realizing

realizing
        that surely
        something was

voice

there is a soft voice calling
in the distance
that has neither owner
       nor name

it is simply a voice calling

it has no purpose

it has no intention
of moving a person or thing
or of even itself being moved

but we are

it is

that small voice only reciting
the words it has always known
since the beginning of time
and in the softest
and oldest language

       silence

origin

it is from the earth
        that dirt within us
that all things grow

our lives each but that flower
borne of promise
perseverance

                in any morning in the distance
                in all meadow
                any covered seed in the darkness
                still believes in light and sky

but we here
in our own fluttering shadow of day
on our own only same paths traveled
we ever-forget the true clay of ourselves
the manifest fullness of other, all

and it is only in those moments alone
        in the silence
        in the darkness
that we each remember
to feel within that piece of all
to become threaded to and with again

                on this earth
                we are indeed adhered
                to this soil below us

but it is not gravity holding us here

we are held here more firmly instead
in this ever-wrapping ourselves
around
        through
and within
that intricately interwoven root of all

A modified version of this poem was originally created in response to a piece of fibre artwork by Janet Elliot and hung beside it in the 2014 Kingston WritersFest 'Stitch and Stanza' collaborative display featuring a group of poets and fibre artists.

a long-ago memory revisited

at my own physio this morning
        still waiting to go in
i looked down the hallway
and watched a young girl
hug her mother as she
came out from her own

and i was thrown back
at least a handful of decades
as spontaneously a memory from
very deep within grew new flesh

my sister and i
        she then seven
            three years younger than i
sitting in a hospital's waiting room
again
this perhaps the sixth night in a row

sitting that night and
looking out the lobby window
i watched an evening still full of itself
with its headlights and streetlamps
and neon lights in the darkness
people walking and chatting outside

all of it more cinema than real life
within this windowsill'ed frame
its curtained border
bright lights and low motion
projecting from the outside in
as if from an endless reel
glass turned then to theatre screen

Barb and i each with our books
our parents on some floor above
my grandmother there
        still gravely ill

i remember asking when we arrived
if we could also go upstairs to visit
and was firmly told again 'no'

i merely accepted it
i then too young to challenge
or even question
        but today i realize
             it wasn't the 'hospital policy'
            we were told that night
and believe it was instead
more their decision to not allow
us to tarnish our young memories
of her with this

so i read my books
watched my sister
        reading hers
i don't remember us talking much

i remember at one point
closing the book and
lifting my eyes finally from it
to take in the shape of the room
watching people come and go
and i wondered about them
and felt sorry for what they
seemed to be going through

i remember then looking toward
the sound of elevator doors
opening and finally this time
seeing my parents inside

my mother still trying to hide
that she'd been weeping
my father always stoic
but i could sense an emptiness
a blankness in his eyes

no words were spoken

this moment beyond words

and as i picked up our books
took my sister's hand and knew
we would not ever
be coming back

veil of day

in a billion stitches per second
the universe with its fine needle
weaves lives and time together
delicately
intrinsically

and in those few instants
of our own clarity after
only then are we able and
allowed to touch the full
of the fabric
of that woven veil

the full of you

you are not simply
        the person
you think you are

your body
your mind
your voice
your breath
your blood

        coursing

you are as much
what you leave
in your passing

your reflected images
your shadows
and your echoes

        left behind

waterways

tying into the wetness
of this fluid stream
      of seconds

and i now already sense
the next thing
      coming

this effortless swim
away from your world
      of distraction

until even the heartbeat of
that noise is silenced

and there is nothing here now
but this calm steady water

and as i stand beside
with my hand upon this surface
of liquid time

i can feel both
the true vastness
      of its ocean

and equally the fullness
of each single droplet
      of wetness within

downtown – may 9th

5:30am
the sun just rising

i am out on the street
already walking

then just in front of me
like an early morning
frightened feral cat
        first peering out from
        its hideout behind bushes
            and buildings
       still daring to leave
a lady emerges
dressed in black
and steps out of shadow
       into morning
steps out of the darkness
       of her life
steps out of a deeper darkness
        beneath the scars of self

i have seen her before
quite often even

she always the same
ankle length black dress
black coat black hat
       even in summer

with always a white pale emptiness
stretched across the full of her face

i believe there was once a time
when she laughed
and danced and sang but
      she lost herself
her place
her name to
those vicious cuts left
by the sometimes razored
      edge of life

and now the pain behind

the pain behind those scars
remains   reminds   demands
that she will never forget

and with the sun early still
this morning
she is already retreating
      to the back of buildings
      in the hidden bushes there

and alone in it
she will whisper her own songs
to herself
in both the languages of
      feral cat

      and shadow

sliver

dusk
hidden slivers of light
in this still expanding
      darkness

this now greying day losing
its once semi-bright lustre

              the other side of the world
              in these past hours shared
              having grown through
                      its own black wonder

dusk
ever elusive

as the closer we get
      it ever-moving
just a step farther away

dusk on its ever-forward
trundling wheels
endlessly tries
to catch up with
and discover dawn

until believing
enough
      becomes it

a winter landscape
after Jacob van Ruisdael's painting 'Winter Landscape' (1660's)

on a very late summer afternoon
as i make my way ever so slowly
through an art gallery
admiring and studying them
        as i normally would until
i come upon one this first time and
i stand here now mesmerized
and beneath my breath i offer
these long-whispered questions
back to you the artist there

back into that very instant before your
already stretching arm and hand
reached to bring your paint-laden brush
in a first stroke against a white patch of canvas

did you paint this from a once-memory?

or were you sitting or standing and
watching this image grow before and
        into you
from a hill just beside and above?

or for you was this not simply an idea
an observation
but instead a vision, arriving?

then coming full
becoming
        the magic
        in your brush
taking anyone who sees this then
        to that original place

a surreal journey back

this winter landscape
losing nothing to season
    or time

and i stand here tonight
lost in this scene
in this painted landscape
    of time long gone and
it drawing my eyes in

past the figures
    in the foreground
the house
    just behind

into the clouds
    above

atop the snow-covered
    earth below

following

following the landscape
    the darkened fields behind
spilling endless into sky

this horizon-less passage

there is no end
as deeper and deeper it goes
    i follow

and as my feet lift from the floor
and follow my eyes
        i leave this world

i blend
becoming fully immersed within
sliding through its set paint
now becoming wet, fluid

becoming
then the damp cold winter air
of 350 years ago

and i in it walk into
        then through

believing now this
landscape painting
        a portal in time
and discovering then
        there is no white
        canvas behind

when asked on your road to silence

when asked
to write
about 'a glass bowl
    of fruit on a table'

write instead
about
    soil
    and sky
    moisture
    and root

about
    mica
    and heat
    and form

about
    diminishing forest
    fallen and
    severed tree

when commanded
alternately then
to write
about 'simply an idea
of a glass bowl
    of fruit on a table'

write instead
about
    ambivalence
    self-serving manifestation
    eco-ignorance
    and fragmented truth

when demanded
then after
to write
about 'the theory
of a glass bowl
    of fruit on a table'

write instead
about
    passive and silent
    observation

about
    the unfathomable distance
    between sight or sound
    and pen
        or thought
        or heart

about
    the endless soft
    and image-laden utterings
    in the fullness of silence

and then
about
    the faltering
    and failing life
    of word

and the ever
and ultimate simplicity
and audaciousness
    of language

on learning

how many days
or weeks or years
      decades even
does it take
for us to learn
a single thing

a lifetime
      perhaps

and that then
carried out the last door
      as we leave

and in that
      echo and dust
ricocheting and settling
      after behind
comes then the new life
the ever-next generations
arriving in their newer flesh

and they at birth
listening to and then
softly whispering back
the first few words
of an echo heard

pulse

it is not that
        staccato
heartbeat within
as much as it is
that steady
        symphonic
metered rhythm
of shared heartbeat

        between

light snow

snow
silent
gently falling
      dancing
catching
the low light
of street lamps

it wears that light
to the ground

then sleeps
      on two sides
            of softness

invisible

to be a hand-sized rock
sharp and jagged
on a very small
beach of fine sand

and in a truest test
of modesty
and humility
becomes
        invisible

needs no definition

as long as my feet stick to the ground
i don't really need to know there is
      a law of gravity
      a law for gravity

i don't really need to know
there is a term for
or a definition of it

and i don't really even
need to know there is gravity

i watch
i observe
i don't feel the need to
equate or give names to that

and 'law of gravity'?

what kind of law is it
that only tells me about
the weight and pull
of and on an object
but cannot calculate
the gravity of the day
      or despair
the gravity of a situation
      of an unfinished word
      of an unfinished story

or the gravity
both behind and ahead
in an
      unfinished life

fear

perhaps

this fear that some
and even i
sometimes share
      of aging
      then death
no different than

ice fearing
becoming
    water
      then vapour

      and then
      invisible

a café in time
> *after Rumi's quote 'Sell your cleverness,
> and buy bewilderment.'*

a café
a coffeehouse on campus

my body appears the oldest here
but the life-force within me
is not

i purposely sit at the lone table
below the café's broken
stopped and frozen
huge wall clock

we both
       it
         and i
timeless

we both
given up believing
in minutes or hours
      even days

a clock still finding its way
in this newness here
i, the last of what's left behind

here in this room above the faces
at the tables there are images
      sounds and colours
all swimming floating
with words riding their ripples
and waves above

it has become my job
my journey
to no longer feel the need
        to create
but to instead simply
        transcribe

i'll leave creation
to the well-educated
        the clever

i've already walked through
that country
and left it

discovered instead a true
and cleaner
        air
        breath
        and life
on this side here

my footprints on the other
        there
the only thing left of me

and even they now covered
trod upon
and already
                      forgotten

this late in autumn   an elegy
for Leonard Cohen

Mr. Cohen,
Leonard,

there is still motion here
on this ascribed last mild day of autumn
before tomorrow's winter air approaches

and in this splintering of season
there is now a spirit
      missing

the colour here began to leave
the day you left this earth

three days before we
finally heard the news
you left us

and on that
third day back
      still unaware
i walked alone
in a quiet park
watching the leaves
as if en masse

             fall

and in that almost silence
i could hear the music of leaves
as they willowed against a breeze
in their slow-dance fall

their notes and chords
barely audible

        but your *Hallelujah*
        softly filled the air

that day of falling leaves
the then almost barren trees
opening up
revealing
        a larger sky
allowing
        perhaps your face
        to be seen
one last time
        in a fading sun

and the leaves
remembering
a gravity greater
        than we know
loosened their hold
to share their colour
with the earth below

these scattered leaves
        multicolored
having already choreographed
themselves in their fall
arranged themselves upon the earth
in a perfect and patterned tribute
to this late autumn day

this year
this day
        your last
leaves having laid themselves out

in their own language

in their last poem
        for you

on this late autumn day

passing

shadow, memory's echo

the remains
of who we are
who we were
what we leave behind

what others take with them
    or let go

we are both action
and inaction
    taken
    left
not in the structures of day
but in the cracks between

we are less than
but equal to
the sum of all

if we are humble
we are greater
than we believe

all on our way to that next crossing
that next thing becoming
before we ourselves
become but
    evening shadow
      a captured echoed voice
      and a fleeting whiff of air

a murder of crows

the past week already having felt
        like early winter
today is though the winter solstice
that official first day
this shortest day of the year

snow already on the ground

though pathways and sidewalks
are passible still

it is now well into dusk
with the slightest bit of light
        yet hanging
onto the low-lying clouds

here as i walk home
just overhead
comes a low-flying small mass
from just behind of something
in that moment undistinguishable
in this low light
but still contrasting in full black
        against a low lustre white

then for me the first focused image
of that black mass fully arriving
only fifteen feet to my side
perhaps only thirty feet above
this ball of black reveals itself
as twenty magnificent crows in flight

and as i look over my shoulder
i see then right behind comes
another twenty more
then more and more and more

in the end perhaps 200 crows in all

their short flight after they pass
then lighting into
two huge barren maple trees
just ahead as i approach

then simultaneously and instantly
as the last of them lands
the hanging low-light on the clouds
        disappears
and a full black of night fills the sky

almost in silhouette
almost in shadow
almost invisible in the trees
they in silence then
as if in the quietest of communal prayer
their own way of remembrance
their humble reverence
knowing what they have just done
in flight

pulling behind them
        the end of light
        the end of day
        the end of season
        this almost end of year

within a day

lost in these days
        mesmerized
by their beauty
their meticulously
orchestrated
        movements

seeing in each instant
        then all
a movement within

and it wasn't for me
always this way

that journey once
edging the jagged rocks
those steep
and treacherous paths
that ever-incline on ledges
barely passable
and i terrified
sometimes
paralyzed

but i now sit in this valley
in this meadow
        old

it the first meadow
of time
where the colour
        green
first perceived itself as real as

all other colour around
believed then fully in
and placed itself there

that green here
in this meadow
this meadow resting beside a lake

the oldest lake
in the world

this lake so full
its stillness then ripple
crest
current always beneath
and its own colours
everchanging
with an even older sun
shimmering

a lake forgetting nothing
saying only seemingly not
what it knows

quiet in its fullness of surface
and depth of days

remembering even
its oldest memory
once but a droplet of water
arriving here

from
         nowhere that it knew

in whispered language of ash and bone

does our dust
        remember?

the fullness
of its former 'other'
once?

does the dust of bone
still hold somewhere within
a once living body's
memories?

its triumphs?
its sorrows?

what is left
in these fragments
        of us?

what dust
of dust
do we leave
        behind?

and what stories
to tell
        after all is done
in whispered
language of
        ash and bone?

rising tides

a rising tide
simply foreplay
between

        bodies of water
        and the gravity of
        the moon

poets

how many poets
does it take to change
a light bulb?

all of them

moving through light and darkness

walk outside the lines
the roads
the paths

colour beyond
boundary

lift the pen from the page
only when you sleep

and then
even in your sleep
even in your dreams
raise your finger
in the darkness
find in it
that faint wet paint
of this passed day's
      shades of light

and with your finger
now dipped within
yesterday's paint
trace the already living ghost a poem
      of tomorrow

this evening
after William Stafford's 'Being a Person'
and W. S, Merwin's 'The Blind Seer of Ambon'

William Stafford
    '...How you stand here is important. How you
    listen for the next things to happen. How you breathe.'
and W. S. Merwin
    '...so this is the way I see now
    I take a shell in my hand
    new to itself and to me
    I feel the thinness the warmth and the cold
    I listen to the water
    which is the story welling up
    I remember the colors and their lives
    everything takes me by surprise
    it is all awake in the darkness'

i who understand
so little   of any
    thing

i who remember
so little
    more

there is an incredible
beauty in this

each day new
exciting
filled with wonder
awe

in it this evening i am brought back
to two small excerpts from poems
written by two of my favourite poets

and in these
and in this evening
       this is how i am

William Stafford's 'Being a Person' appeared in his 'Even in Quiet Places'
(Confluence Press, 2010)

W. S. Merwin's 'The Blind Seer of Ambon' appeared in his 'Travels'
(Alfred A. Knopf, 1994)

almost winter

still on this edge
of the snow coming

late this season
this the first cold morning

we sit here in this café
in comfort
        relative
watching from the inside out

our early morning jaunt
already done

noticed in it
that then slight bite of air
reminder of season's edge

now looking out into the full
grey cloud sky content
        both it
        and i
watching

as if coming from nowhere

from only seemingly nothing

the first snowflake
this season
        falls

stream

under a black and white sky
on this overcast day
clouds only almost breaking
but remaining instead
to carry with them a premonition
of cold and icy rain or snow

lake ontario
its edge only an arm's length away

the white ice covers it
as far as one can see but
just beside this snowy shore
water but a few feet wide
surprises itself open
through and into its rippled grey

winter giving up its grip

this small band of water
the tiniest of silent stream
just waking after rolling so long
beneath itself
and ice

this tiny stream slow and wanting
to be more
to become full spirit
of that grander body

a small stream wishing this morning
to reveal its true self as lake

midwinter

late january
midwinter
        at best

a late afternoon
in this shortness of days

no breeze
a stillness

a walk within

there is nothing in this air
but a light mist
        almost ice
        almost snow

no sound

no sound
but blades on ice
        in a near distance

a leafless small willow
sits in both the season's
and its own nakedness

but as i approach
        almost disbelieving
i notice on it
these still wet enveloped
        almost ice-encased
buds
calling out to be touched
as if to confirm
they are real

languages

dead winter
in a large open room
a fireplace sits
        empty
        cold

a heart in
another room
another house
another place
sits
        the same

what is the language
of fire?

again on aging

on the downside
of the hill
of life

        as if life
        were a hill

lost
in an almost
slow
        motion
                roll

a gentle glide

neither
calculated
nor planned

in this last
dance
this final
tango

that easy
that simple
first the watching
the listening then
for as long as
the music lasts

the slow
embraced

        swaying

what i mostly am

i have become mostly
an observer
      passive

my life played out
like a film
      and i it's only
audience
      at ease
      comfortable
      content

i am a fly on the wall

no, i am an idea
      of a fly on the wall

no, i am an idea of an idea
      of an idea

no, mostly
i am the first letter
of the first word
of an idea
      unsure

from last night

i was going to write a poem
about something i thought last night
but i have forgotten what it was

instead here on this table
in front of me
this blank page

with pen in hand
i stare through this
coffeehouse window

i watch the ice covered
docking pond across the street
       first time this winter, late

lake ontario beyond
       rippled
         open and clear

and now here in an instant
last night's poem emerging
anew and visual
visceral

the docking pond
       last night's page

gardens

...again this morning that faint sound
you always hear in this place...

elevated just slightly to your right
you'll notice again that same small
well-tilled garden you see each day
on your walk past

you will believe you know it well
and you do

the same rows of tulips
the intermittent batches
        of daises chrysanthemums
        small ferns and other bushes
        for which you have no name
the occasional small bunny
you've seen quite often but
        still never enough
the squirrels the chipmunks
the bees hovering above and
        that same faint as if musical
        but haunting sound
you always hear as you pass

a sound
        unique
you cannot describe
and this the only place
you've ever heard it
you ever hear it still...

how
> *after William Stafford's 'Being a Person'*

how we grow
how we lay our feet down
how we walk through
this world is important

how we neglect
        or caress
a day
        more

there is a life-force within you
hard
simultaneously soft
        waiting
to absorb each of the all
arriving

unbounded and endless
cascades
ever-crossing before you

with eclectic array
of image and sound

as your earth and day grows
your echoes
your footprints
how solid
        but softly still

William Stafford's 'Being a Person' appeared in his 'Even in Quiet Places'
(Confluence Press, 2010)

here

here
this one life

this breath

today
this first true day of spring
beneath a half-forgotten sun

still this chilly breeze
reminder yet
       of season past

these freeze-frame moments
in frozen time

their whispers
and shadows falling
on shivering
       twigs and
       open buds

the snow of days behind

the languages of history

how this afternoon
describes this morning
is written
      will be told
in a more ancient language
than
how tomorrow
will describe
today

in that hidden garden behind

…that sound willows from
behind and below
and there
at the edge of that small and
hidden garden
a simple mother robin
      stands
and watches silent
as beside her on the ground

her dead fledgling
      sings

in the end

in the end
i will have been
writing a single poem
        for over seventy-five years

words written
        in blood
on a
        parchment of days

my tears
        lines between stanzas

my laughter
        punctuation missing

my breath
        the space between words

my sighs
        longer spaces
        indented lines

my thoughts
        ever-erased
        before my ink/blood
        reached the page

in the end
                        in the end

when this all ceases

when the first shovelful of earth
falls on some container of body
lying at the bottom of a freshly dug grave

look away
walk away
find in the morning light
      in the night sky
your own parchment
      of days
upon which your own words
are already being written

place your hand on the open
and only ever-page
      of today

and with your other open palm
out in front of you
touch the slight breeze
gaze to the sky
then back to the earth

simply watch
and listen
and in it sense
the heartbeat of
      all the dead
      and the living
and beneath even it
that fainter heartbeat of
      the all of that yet unborn

    in the end

        in the end

on this shore

here on this shore
there is no shortage
of either image
or ink

but
when i run out of paper
i will with a stick
sketch poems
in the soil
until all untouched earth
is gone

when i run out of soil
i will then with a finger
draw my poems
on tracings of air

and when i run out of air

About the Author

Bruce Kauffman lives in Kingston and is a local poet, editor, and organizer of literary events. In addition to his collaborative work with other artists, his written work has appeared in several anthologies and journals, broadsides, two chapbooks, and three collections of poetry, with *an evening's absence still waiting for moon* his fourth. Beyond writing and editing, he organizes occasional book launch or reading events, facilitates intuitive writing workshops, founded, organizes and hosts the monthly 'and the journey continues' open mic reading series, the annual multiday Poets @ Artfest poetry festival, and Kingston's tie to the global 100 Thousand Poets for Change held annually. He also produces and hosts his weekly spoken word radio show, 'finding a voice', on CFRC 101.9fm.

About the Cover Photographer

Ali Dixon is a fourth year Film and Media Major at Queen's University in Kingston Ontario. Her photography, both film and digital, have been shown in the Unit 115 Kingston Arts Council Gallery Space for the exhibition, "But Six Moments in the All of Time" along side poems by Bruce Kauffman.

Her photography is an eclectic mix of observational realism and causal experimentation. She hopes to create a portfolio of fine art photography in the future.

Ali is also very interested in working with film photography and has explored 35mm film photography techniques and self-developing methods over the past year in her studies. She hopes to work with larger formats and learn to fully process her own film and prints in the near future.

Her photography and art can be viewed on her Instagram: @aliemdixon

www.ingramcontent.com/pod-product-compliance
Lightning Source LLC
Chambersburg PA
CBHW020128130526
44591CB00032B/571